Waiting in Hope

Reflections on Advent

Tony Flannery

First published 2002 by
Veritas Publications
7/8 Lower Abbey Street
Dublin 1
Ireland
Email publications@veritas.ie
Website www.veritas.ie

ISBN 1 85390 667 0

A catalogue record for this book is available from the British Library.

Designed by Colette Dower
Cover photograph by Dave Keegan
Printed in the Republic of Ireland by Betaprint Ltd, Dublin

*Veritas books are printed on paper made from the wood pulp of managed
forests. For every tree felled, at least one tree is planted, thereby renewing
natural resources.*

CONTENTS

1

Expectancy and Waiting

It is probably true that the season of Advent doesn't mean very much to the average Catholic. It occurs during those hectic weeks before Christmas, when everything is a rush, and there is a sense of excitement in the air. The regular Sunday Mass attender will hear about Advent during the four Sundays before Christmas, but usually it doesn't impinge deeply on his or her consciousness. This book is an attempt to help believers, whether they be church-going or not, to find some meaning in this season.

In many ways it is the loveliest season of what we call the Church's year. If you try to enter into the season of Advent it will repay you abundantly, helping you to come to a deeper and more soundly based understanding of your faith, and a better knowledge of that person who was expected, and who we believe has come as our Saviour.

There are two basic themes or ideas that are central to Advent. The first one is the idea of expectancy. The Jews were hoping for a saviour. As the Gospel puts it:

A spirit of expectancy had grown among the people...

In order to have this feeling of expectancy, we must first be aware of the need for something, or someone, new in our lives. We must have some sense of our emptiness, our inadequacy, maybe even our sinfulness. At the very least we must be aware of our need for some form of new life, of salvation. To help yourself develop this consciousness you could spend some time on Psalm 62, the great expression of our need for God.

> *O God, you are my God, for you I long;*
> *For you my soul is thirsting.*
> *My body pines for you*
> *Like a dry weary land without water.*
> *So I gaze on you in the sanctuary*
> *To see your strength and your glory.*

I think that some awareness of our need is deep in the hearts and minds of most of us. We probably try to avoid thinking about it too much because it can be painful. But deep down we long for life, for love, for a feeling of permanence, the assurance that in the midst of all that is passing away, we might live on in some form or other. And that the love we experience in this life might last beyond the grave.

So this is not too difficult an idea to relate to, even if it is painful to stay with. We are longing for a saviour, and Advent tells us to look forward with hope to His coming.

The second big theme of Advent is waiting. This one is more difficult for us who live in the modern world. We have become used to everything being quickly available, and easily disposable. It is an instant age in which we live. The idea of waiting patiently while something grows slowly in the darkness is foreign to most of us, except for those who still like to cultivate their garden, and are in touch with the cycles of nature. During Advent we have to learn that God works by a different time scale to ours. As St Peter, in his letter, says:

> *…with the Lord a day can mean a thousand years, and a thousand years is like a day…*

One of the striking images of Advent is Mary, the pregnant young girl. As the days and weeks pass slowly, the life of God is growing within her. It has to be an anxious, uncertain time for her, and yet a time of deep pondering on the mystery. She must have wondered greatly what sort of child was growing within her, and longed for it to be born. But, as any pregnant woman must know well, the processes of nature cannot be rushed. They have to be allowed to take their course. She must learn to be patient, to wait.

In the same way we too must learn patience in our dealings with God. He is growing in our lives too, slowly and imperceptibly, like the darkness and stillness of the womb. We have to learn to wait, to get in tune with the rhythms of God, and adjust our lives to them. This is part of what we try to do in Advent.

The purpose of this little book is to take the central Advent themes, and to present them in a way that is simple and easy to grasp, and in a way that relates to the living of our ordinary lives in the modern world. I will use the readings from the Masses of the season, especially the four Sundays. I will particularly refer to the passages from the Prophet Isaiah. If you are not familiar with the Old Testament, try not to allow the strangeness of the language and images to put you off too quickly. The writings of Isaiah are wonderful and beautiful, as you will gradually discover if you can stay with them. But they need a little perseverance. Read them as you would poetry, which is really what they are. Allow the images to speak to your mind and heart. Like any good poem, they will mean different things to different people. Don't look for 'official' or 'correct' interpretations. Let God use them to say to you whatever he wants you to hear, whatever message of love he knows is needed in your life.

This book is not intended to be read through in one sitting. Dip into it during the weeks of Advent. Take a little time over it. Ponder the Scripture passages. If a passage strikes you, spend anything up to ten or fifteen minutes just repeating it slowly and gently in the silence, letting it sink into your heart. You might find that you end up staying with one or two passages for the four weeks. That is fine too. There is no one exclusive way of pondering the mystery of God and praying to him. Everyone finds their own way.

The phrase, or prayer, that best sums up the meaning of Advent is what has come to be known as the 'Jesus Prayer'. You might be able to make it part of your life, part even of your breathing, during these weeks:

Come, Lord Jesus.

2

GOD: A JOURNEY OF DISCOVERY

Perhaps a bit of background would be useful before we get into the Advent readings themselves.

During the course of each year, the Church, through it's different liturgies, tries to celebrate the whole story of our salvation. It goes from the creation of the world, using the marvellous mythological stories of the Book of Genesis, the first book of the Bible, through the slow and gradual development of the Jewish people's understanding of God, until the final revelation, which is the coming of Jesus.

At first the Jewish notion of God was primitive. He was exclusively their God, his only brief being to look after them. Other nations had different gods, but the Jews considered themselves special because their God was more powerful than the gods of the other nations. He fought with them in their battles. Their enemies were his enemies. All this seems fairly primitive to us now, but it fitted well into the culture and beliefs of the time. Nobody had yet come to the notion of an all-powerful God of all creation.

Over the centuries Jewish teachers and prophets gradually came to new and deeper understandings of God. They tried to teach these new notions to the people, and get them to integrate them into their belief. It wasn't always easy. Probably the idea the people found most difficult to accept was that God did not belong to them alone, but was equally the God of other nations. They hadn't got any exclusive claim on him. The problem this created was clear and very practical. If he was the God of all nations, was there any guarantee that He would fight with them in their wars? If they couldn't be sure that He was on their side in battle, there was no longer a guarantee of victory. What was the point of having a God at all, if he wasn't on their side and against their enemies?

The other big adjustment that had to be made was the realisation that God was not a warlike God, but that He was a God of peace, that He wanted people to live harmoniously with each other. I suppose you could argue that the Jews never quite learned that lesson. But then, did any of the Christian nations learn it either? It is a hard lesson.

Gradually, as the centuries passed, a new and beautiful image of God began to emerge among the Jewish people. Not everyone accepted or believed in this sort of God. Old notions die hard, as we know in our own time. But some of the really wise people, especially those who wrote the book we know as the Book of the Prophet Isaiah, presented an image of God that, even to this day, can inspire and excite people with the wonderful hope and promise that it contains. These writings are central to the Advent season.

The Jews believed from earliest times that God would send a messenger, a saviour. The name they gave this promised messenger was the Messiah, the one who was to come. The writings of the Old Testament prophets contain many predictions about this messenger, and the reign or way of life that he would initiate in the world when he arrived. Gradually expectations built up. The later books of the Old Testament, especially, have a vibrant sense of hope and promise. In some ways we could envy the people of those times, living with a strong feeling of expectation of a future that would be wonderful beyond their imaginings. If you believe with a great degree of certainty, as they did, that the future would be much greater than the present, then life takes on a deep meaning. With that sort of belief some of the problems that plague our society today, like suicide, or the many emotional and depressive illnesses we encounter, would not be so common. Those people had hope. They had something to look forward to.

The story of the Jewish people and their search for God, as outlined in the Old Testament, is in a real sense the story of all of us. Every believer goes through a journey and a struggle in their effort to come to know God in their lives. For most of us the discovery of God is gradual and slow. We must learn to be patient. Often we have to unlearn false notions that we picked up along the way. Unlearning the past is usually far more difficult than learning something new. Many of the older generation have had to unlearn harsh images of God that were given to us as children, images of a God who is distant, cold and judgemental. We grew up in an era when the judgement of God was emphasised much more than his mercy and love. We learned to fear him. It is hard to free ourselves from that. Fear is an instinct that comes easily to humans. It feeds into our insecurity and uncertainty. It can eat away at our faith and hope, and take the joy out of our lives.

In the weeks of Advent the Church tries to help us to relive the expectation and hope of the Jewish people before Jesus. That is why the Old Testament readings, and especially the Book of Isaiah, play such a big part in the Masses and liturgies of these weeks. The idea is that we try to enter into the mood and feeling of the people of the time. The expected messenger hadn't yet come. The promise was not yet fulfilled. As we have seen, they were still struggling with their notion of God. We are asked to enter into this struggle with them. But they were also full of hope. And to be part of the celebration of Advent is to be a person of hope.

There are two major obstacles preventing us from entering into the Advent mood and atmosphere. Firstly, Christ, and his coming, are so much a part of our lives that we find it hard to get excited about it. Most of us have grown up believing that he has come and saved us. The promise has been fulfilled. And maybe we don't even feel that His coming has made much difference. The ordinary effort and drudgery of life continues.

We have to try to stand back and look again at this Messiah, and the promise he brought. We must accept that while Christ has come into the world, there are many ways in which we haven't allowed him into our own lives. Through living the weeks of Advent we may get some insight into what is blocking his presence, what it is in us that is preventing his coming as our personal Lord and Saviour.

The second thing that makes Advent hard for us is that as a society we begin to celebrate Christmas anything up to two months before it arrives. This is something that none of us as individuals have much control over, but it is a great pity. The weeks that the Church has designated for Advent, the three or four weeks before Christmas, are increasingly a time of parties and celebrations of all sorts. When you are already anticipating the event, it is next to impossible to enter into the mood of waiting and expectation. Maybe the first essential step in celebrating Advent adequately is to postpone, as far as possible, the Christmas festivities until it actually arrives, or at least until a few days beforehand.

Give time and space for the sense of expectancy and longing to develop within you.

Come, Lord Jesus.

3

THE WORK OF HIS HANDS

If Advent is to be a time of expectation, a time of waiting in hope for a messenger to come, then it is essential that we are aware of our need. In today's world it is easy to get lost in the rush, in the ready access to material things, to enjoyment and pleasure. 'The world is sick, because people do not think' said Pope Paul V1 many years ago. There is a truth in what he says. We can get caught up in the frenetic pace of it all, and only realise how empty our lives are when we meet with a crisis.

So, the first essential for celebrating Advent is to slow down, to take time to think; to realise that our hearts have deep longings that no material possession, no power, prestige or influence, can satisfy.

As I said earlier, try not to let the language and images of Isaiah, which come from a very ancient time, put you off. When you get used to them, and begin to read his words as poetry, you will discover great riches in them. He can express the frailty and weakness of our lives very powerfully in one image:

> *We are all like withered leaves*
> *And our sins blow us away like the wind...*

Take time to enter into the image of the withered leaf. Have you ever felt that sense of uselessness, that sense that life is short, futile and aimless; that you are just blown around by chance; that the world is big, hostile and frightening, and you are a puny little being in the midst of it all? And in your weakness and failure you feel helpless and afraid. It is good to let these feelings come to us at times. They bring us down to earth, rid us of our stupid pride. And, most of all, they open us to the awareness of something greater. The danger of getting lost in the hectic pace of modern life is that our world will grow narrow. We will come to believe that there is nothing beyond what we experience in our day to day living. And then, when the crisis comes that throws our life out of kilter, we are left without the resources to deal with it.

So it is good to experience the feeling of the withered leaf, blowing around in the wind. But Isaiah immediately comes to our rescue;

> And yet, Lord, you are our Father:
> We the clay, you the potter,
> We are all the work of your hand.

These are marvellous lines, if we come to them from the perspective of the withered leaf. Life takes on a new meaning. We are opened up to a wonderful vista of possibility. Instead of emptiness, futility, aimlessness, now everything is possible, because we are all the work of his hand, and he is shaping us each day like the potter shapes the clay. During the early part of Advent, try to rest for a while every now and again with that image. You are the work of his hand. Begin to feel the wonder of it, the new sense of your worth and value. And you will come to know the meaning of that most commonly used sentence in the whole of the Bible: do not be afraid.

The other big theme from the early readings of Advent is the notion of being alert. St Paul expresses it:

The time has come; you must wake up now…
The night is almost over; it will be daylight soon.

It took me time and work to really appreciate that passage. If you have the image of a fearful, judgmental God in your mind or heart, it can be a frightening sentence, and some passages in the Gospel lend themselves to that interpretation. St Luke has Jesus talking about fearful signs and great distress. But these are very much eclipsed by the overall theme. The time that is coming is not a time of darkness, but of daylight, a time of opportunity, when the potter will shape us to his image. Like all growth and development, the work of the potter will involve some pain and distress, but the ultimate aim is life, not death. And that is the crucial thing. This time it is the prophet Jeremiah who expresses it:

See, the days are coming… when I am going to fulfil the promise I made.
In those days Judah will be saved
And Israel shall dwell in confidence.

We are now at the central core of Advent, and indeed of our faith. It is something that we need to work on, so that we will be totally clear about it. The one we are waiting for, whose coming we are expecting, whose promise is being fulfilled, is not a dealer in death and destruction. He is the Life Giver. We can be burdened with negative thoughts both about ourselves and God. It is worth taking time on these texts, repeating them over quietly so that they settle within us and become part of the way we think and feel. This does not happen quickly or easily. Coming to know God, growing in confidence in his love for us, is a life-long task. But Advent is a time to be patient.

The whole message of this early part of Advent is summed up beautifully in the words of Jesus from St Luke's Gospel:

When these things begin to take place, stand erect, hold your head high, because your liberation is near at hand.

And that, most of all, is the image to stay with. These are the words to repeat over and over. Our liberation is at hand.

So we begin Advent, aware of our own weakness and failure, and yet full of hope and confidence because the days are coming, and the promise will be fulfilled. We can stand erect and hold our heads high. He, the life-giver, will come and set us free.

4

THE KINGDOM OF GOD

Repent, for the Kingdom of God is at hand.

That was the theme of John the Baptist's preaching. And we are told that Jesus, when he stood up in the synagogue in Gallilee to give his first talk, repeated the same words:

The time is near; the Kingdom of God is at hand; repent and believe the Good News.

The scholars, who have done so much to open up the meaning of the Bible for us in the past thirty years or so, tell us that everything Jesus said from then on was really a drawing out, an explanation, of that opening talk.

Did you ever wonder if Jesus knew who he was and what the purpose of his life was, from the first moment of his birth? Did he open his eyes in the stable in Bethlehem and say to himself: 'Here I am, the Son of God, come to save the world'? Probably not. In fact the general opinion among scholars today is that he only gradually came to a realisation of his identity and his mission. Most people, as they go on in life, grow in self-knowledge and understanding of the meaning of their lives. It probably happened in somewhat the same way with Jesus. We know that he was a perceptive and clear-thinking person, and during his developing years he must have observed life and people closely, and began to form his message. At the same time he 'grew in wisdom, age and grace', and as he came to know God more fully through prayer and reflection, he began to understand who he was. Around the age of thirty he was ready. He knew himself and knew he had something to say, so he stood up one day in the local synagogue, and made that statement.

> *The time is near; the Kingdom of God is at hand; repent, and believe the Good News.*

The 'Kingdom of God' was the name Jesus gave to his vision of a new way of life, a new way for people to relate to each other and to God. There are three central planks, or core values, to this vision.

> *Instead of all the war and conflict people should live at peace with each other.*
> *Instead of hatred, divisions and bitterness, people should learn to love each other.*
> *Instead of inequality and injustice, every human person should be given a fair deal in life.*

When Jesus used the word 'repent' it had a somewhat different meaning for his listeners than it does for us today. This brings us to a central problem in understanding the Bible, the difficulty of interpreting the precise meaning of a language that is no longer used. It is one of the areas where scholars have made great progress, and they can now give us a clearer picture of what exactly Jesus meant.

So, what did the word 'repent' mean for Jesus and his listeners? It had to do with looking at things in a new way, taking a new perspective on life. Basically he was trying to tell people that the way they were living, the way in which the world was organised, was foolish and destructive. Wars, hatred, inequality brought misery and unhappiness to people's lives. If they could begin to see things in a new way, then they could live by different values, and the world would become a happier and a better place. The 'Kingdom of God' that he talked about was most of all a new way of looking at things, a new way of thinking about ourselves and the world around us. It didn't relate only to the next life. It was a vision of how life could be lived here and now. And having come into being in the present it would find its fulfilment in eternity.

So, this vision of Jesus, this Kingdom of God, is something for us to engage with during these weeks. He didn't come to install it in its completed form, but to initiate it, and to strengthen and empower us to do our bit in bringing it to fruition. If we are waiting for his coming, full of expectancy of the new life that he is bringing, then we must be prepared to try to live by the values of his Kingdom.

As John the Baptist said:

Prepare a way for the Lord, make his paths straight.

That is very much part of the Advent journey. We prepare the way by living in peace and love and by, in whatever way we can, building a society in which every human being has the opportunity to live a decent life.

There is no one better than Isaiah at painting an image of this new way of life:

The wolf lives with the lamb,
The panther lies down with the kid,
Calf and lion cub feed together
With a little boy to lead them.
The cow and the bear make friends,

Their young lie down together...
They do no hurt, no harm,
On all my holy mountain,
For the country is filled with the knowledge of the Lord
As the waters swell the sea.

This promise for which we are expectantly waiting is not something small or trivial, something that will make little or no difference. On the contrary, it is a whole new way of life, a 'new Heaven and a new Earth'.

5

PROMISE OF NEW LIFE

The reading for the Masses of the second week of Advent are rich with sentences and phrases from Isaiah that are beautiful in their range and depth, and that deserve and repay time in contemplation. In a sweep of different images he paints a picture of the new life, the Kingdom of God.

At the risk of being repetitive can I remind you again not to attempt to interpret any of these passages literally, or even wonder too much about what exactly they mean. Better to let the image stay with you, as you would a poem, and speak more to your heart than to the logical and literal side of your mind. As St Exupery says through the mouth of the Little Prince: 'It is only with the heart that one can see rightly. What is essential is invisible to the eye'.

What better place to begin than the following from Isaiah:

> Console my people, says the Lord, console them.
> Speak to the heart of Jerusalem, and call to her
> That her time of service is ended, and her sin is atoned for...

All hope has to begin somewhere like this. The hurt of the past, the failure to measure up to what you wanted to achieve; the damage done, whether intentional or not; the missed opportunities; all of these can be put aside; they can be overcome. The works of God are wonderful, and more especially for those who are in greatest need.

Let every valley be filled in,
Every mountain and hill be laid low.
Let every cliff become a plain,
And the ridges a valley.

This is very important. For the follower of Jesus, there is always the possibility of new life, new beginning. No matter how inadequate we feel, no matter how hopeless or destructive our past has been, we can start afresh. Everything can be forgiven. This is one of the ways in which our faith differs radically from the accepted views of society. The tendency in society is to judge people and condemn them without any hope of redemption. We see it so often in the tabloid media. Certain people who have done wrong are branded as 'evil', 'beasts' 'utterly corrupt', and the judgement is final. For the Christian, no judgement is final. God loves the sinner, and His love, like Francis Thompson's 'Hound of Heaven', does not give up. The valleys can be filled in, and the mountains and hills laid low. And then, with all the hurt and damage of the past made well again, we can really move on, and look forward with hope.

The Saviour comes to bring new life. This involves a new way of looking at things. Isaiah introduces us to the notion of 'wisdom'. The spirit of the Lord will be:

A spirit of wisdom and insight,
A spirit of counsel and power,
A spirit of knowledge and the fear of the Lord.

So we no longer live in the darkness. It is in darkness that sin and destruction live and flourish. We are now in the daylight, and that is where wisdom can nourish and lead us.

When it comes to describing this new life, Isaiah really lets his imagination loose. And we must do the same. When we deal with the works of God our minds are pathetically inadequate. We cannot understand His ways. We can only glimpse his presence. That is why the great spiritual writers so often fall back on poetic images. Isaiah says that when he comes, the messenger:

> Will hammer their swords into ploughshares,
> And their spears into sickles.
> Nation will not lift sword against nation,
> There will be no more training for war.

Peace is one of the core values of the new life, the Kingdom. This peace will not just embrace humanity, but the whole of creation:

> For God has decreed the flattening of each high mountain,
> Of the everlasting hills,
> The filling of the valleys to make the ground level
> So that Israel can walk in safety under the glory of God.
> And the forest and every fragrant tree will provide shade
> For Israel at the command of God;
> For God will guide Israel in joy by the light of his glory
> With his mercy and integrity for escort.

Don't let the talk of 'Israel' put you off. Read this as applying to ourselves, to every human person, and the whole of creation. It is an image of what is possible, of the new life that God is bringing. If you stay with it, the image can gradually fill your heart with hope for the future of the world, a belief that there is the possibility of a very different way of living. You can begin to hope and trust that it can happen, not just in the promised eternity, but that a beginning can be made right here among us. Some people will dismiss it all as a pipe dream, as fantasy. But so much of the Christian faith is like this. It is based on hope, and trust in the benign working of God among us. Surely it is better to live our lives buoyed up by the promise of a better world, than in a trough of despair about the problems of the present. With hope in our hearts, and a vision to inspire us, it is possible that we might begin to do a little bit to bring that vision about.

When you have made the images of a peaceful creation your own, and have got some sense of excitement about what is possible for humanity, you can move on to the following ringing call from Isaiah.

> Go up on a high mountain, joyful messenger of Zion.
> Shout with a loud voice, joyful messenger of Jerusalem.
> Shout without fear; say to the towns of Judah,
> Here is your God.

So, a reflection that begins with the call of God to 'console my people', and leads us through wonderful images of the Kingdom that is to come, ends in a note of joy, a joy so great that you want to shout it out from the top of a mountain. If contemplation of God, and the promise he offers, can give us even a small share of this joy, then it is time well spent.

And, lastly, we are left with a picture of the nature of God and his relationship with us. He has asked us to console his people; now he wants to console us.

> He is like a shepherd feeding his flock,
> Gathering lambs in his arms,
> Holding them against his breast,
> And leading to their rest the mother ewes.

For those of us who find it hard to feel God close, or who are in any way nervous, afraid or guilty in his presence, there is plenty of food for prayer and contemplation here. Take time to dwell in his presence; allow him to hold you against his breast, and to lead you to rest.

6

Bringing Good News to the Poor

Christianity is a community religion. Many of the Christian churches, especially the more evangelical and fundamentalist ones, tend to gloss over the social teaching of the Bible. They present Christian living as a personal thing. They talk a great deal about sin, but it is personal sin, usually with the emphasis on sexual failures. Their message goes something like this: Repent of your sins, turn to Jesus and be born again, and you will be saved. They use selected Bible quotations to present an Old Testament idea that personal wealth and prosperity are a sign of God's blessing. Maybe that is why they have been so spectacularly successful in parts of the world. As long as a person is living a moral life, in the traditional sense of right living, they can feel comfortable in their wealth. Indeed it is a sign that God approves of them. They are in a sense the new chosen people. Having been born again, and living good lives as they see it, their salvation is secure. Catholicism has often been tainted with these types of attitudes also. And today some strands of charismatic and Marian devotion are very personalised, with little or no social dimension.

I have never been comfortable with the idea that my purpose on earth is to save my soul, to get myself safely up to Heaven. It always seemed a selfish belief to me. I know that the idea of loving and caring for other people was taught, but the slant that was often given was that it was the way we accumulated merit for ourselves. If I loved other people, then God would be pleased with me and reward me with Heaven. The focus was ultimately on myself, and my welfare. I don't believe it any more. I don't know how any of us could be happy in eternity if some of the people with whom we had shared our lives were condemned to Hell. No, I believe we work out our salvation as part of a community, and we try to love each other not because it will benefit ourselves in the end, but because love is the best human response, the proper thing to do. Love, rather than salvation, is the ultimate goal of the follower of Christ. As we saw earlier, one of the core planks of Jesus' vision of the Kingdom was a world in which every human being would have a fair chance in life. So, the message of Isaiah, repeated in their teaching by John the Baptist and Jesus, is a central message of our faith.

> The spirit of the Lord has been given to me,
> For the Lord has anointed me.
> He has sent me to bring good news to the poor,
> To bind up hearts that are broken;
> To proclaim liberty to captives,
> Freedom to those in prison;
> To proclaim a year of favour from the Lord.

The gifts of God, which he showers generously on us, are never given for ourselves alone. They are given to us to be shared, to be spread around. They are given to us particularly so that we can care for the poor. We used to argue a lot about who are the poor. Is it the spiritually poor Jesus was talking about? I don't think so. He meant those who are deprived of the opportunity to live a decent life through social, political or economic circumstances. There is no way around the hard edge of this teaching. So, uncomfortable and all as it may be, we must spend time with these passages.

Then the eyes of the blind shall be opened,
The ears of the deaf unsealed,
Then the lame shall leap like a deer
And the tongues of the dumb sing for joy.

None of this will happen without our being instrumental in bringing it about.

John the Baptist is in prison. While there he has time to think, to wonder. He is hearing all sorts of stories about Jesus, the new prophet. He has spent the last few years announcing the coming of this person, and, as he said himself, preparing the way. He is delighted with what he is hearing, but inevitably, sitting alone in his cell, he begins to question. Is this really the one who is to come? So he sends his disciples to ask Jesus, are you the one? The answer Jesus gives is taken straight from the prophet Isaiah:

Go back and tell John what you hear and see; the blind see again, and the lame walk, lepers are cleansed, and the deaf hear, the dead are raised to life and the Good News is proclaimed to the poor.

Jesus is letting John know in that answer that he is fulfilling the test of any true follower of God, anyone who has received the Spirit of God. He is putting his belief into practice by working for the underprivileged. This is where the real challenge of the faith comes in, and where it can get difficult and uncomfortable. Up to now we have reflected on the wonderful news of God's care for his people:

Of this I am sure, that your love lasts forever...

But now we are told that it is not enough just to bask in that love. We have to spread it around, not only among our own close circle, but across the social and racial divides. We are living in one of the wealthier countries in the world, while large numbers of people live in poverty. In what way can we, as Christians, bring good news to the poor? There are no easy answers, either to the problem of poverty and inequality in the world, or to what the responsibility of each individual Christian should be.

But the question remains.

> *What life have you if you have not life together?*
> *There is no life that is not in community,*
> *And no community not lived in praise of God.*
>   (T. S. Eliot, Choruses from 'The Rock')

It is a hard thing to do, but we must try not to avoid the difficult and challenging aspects of Christian teaching. Unless we are people of love, we are not really the followers of Jesus.

St James puts it: *Faith without works is dead.* And St Paul: *If we have not love, we are nothing.*

Both are clearly speaking, not of a romantic love, but of the hard-nosed love that provokes us into putting ourselves on the line in the service of others. God does not expect us to be perfect in this love. But he does expect us to reach for that ideal.

7

A HAPPY PEOPLE

As we come into the third week of Advent we are in the heart of winter. The winter solstice is just around the corner. The days are short, often dull and grey, with long, dark nights. In our climate it is usually wet and cold. At this time of year many of us are at our most vulnerable. Whatever weaknesses are in our system begin to show up, and we are susceptible to flues and other sicknesses. All the darkness can generate depression, even in people not particularly prone to it.

There is a further reason why this can be a hard time of the year. Christmas is just around the corner. It is supposed to be a time of celebration, and for some the festivities are already in full swing. But others find it a difficult time. The focus is on family, and family celebration. But not all families are happy, or like being together. It may be the only time in the year they come together, and the tension precedes the gathering, while, when they assemble, conflict quickly surfaces and turns the festive season into a miserable few days. Christmas can also renew the pain of broken marriages and families that have split up. Or maybe the problem is that you have no one to share the celebrations with. In that case it can be the loneliest time of the year. For the rest of the year you may be doing fine, but the outburst of celebration gives you the feeling that you are missing something. If you have lost the person you loved, someone with whom you have shared many Christmases but is now dead, all the grief and loneliness can come back to haunt you. Many people long for Christmas to be over.

And yet this third week of Advent the readings are rich with the theme of joy and happiness. With the exception of Easter week, it is probably the most vibrant and joyful week in the whole of the Church calendar. We are called on to be happy, to be people of joy.

To be fair the readings do acknowledge that life is not always a bed of roses, that there is much unhappiness and suffering. But they try to get us to look beneath the surface, to realise that there is a deeper reality to life, and if we can tune in to it, we will find what Jesus called 'a peace beyond all understanding'. Isaiah has words of encouragement for us:

> Strengthen all weary hands,
> Steady all trembling knees
> And say to all faint hearts,
> Courage, do not be afraid.

Here we have it again, that sentence that runs through the Bible, do not be afraid. It is a call for us to rise above our depression, to look beyond our present unhappiness. In spite of all the difficulty of life there is still reason to be joyful:

> Look, your God is coming…
> He is coming to save you.

You may feel miserable, sick in body or depressed. But you are not without hope. Your God is coming to save you.

St Paul is usually solemn in his letters. He does not come across as a particularly light-hearted character. And yet, even he is insistent on the need for joy:

I want you to be happy, always happy in the Lord. I repeat, what I
want is your happiness.

We have a clear message here, and one that we as a Church have
sometimes allowed to slip out of our consciousness. The Christian,
the follower of Christ, is meant to be a happy person.

Rejoice, exult with all your heart,
Daughter of Jerusalem...

The Lord your God is in your midst ...
He will exult with joy over you,
He will renew you by his love;
He will dance with shouts of joy for you...

I exult for joy in the Lord,
My soul rejoices in my God.

Not many of us were brought up with the notion of the Christian as a
joyful, happy person, particularly in the Western Church. We have tended
to see Christian living as a serious business, a matter of life and death. The
emphasis was on avoiding sin and living a good life so that we would save
our souls and get to Heaven. There wasn't much room for fun and
enjoyment, because the task was serious and the stakes were high.
Avoiding mortal sin, and preserving ourselves from the jaws of Hell, were
not exactly laughing matters. Even when we gather in church we are
solemn. We were taught that talking in church was wrong, and
disrespectful to the presence of Jesus. He was not very tolerant of chat
and laughter. We should be quiet and serious in his company. Jesus as
someone who was happy, who had a sense of humour and liked being
with people, is not an idea that sits comfortably with the average Catholic.

I believe this is a problem. Our religion has suffered greatly from being too solemn and serious, from the absence of a sense of fun and joy. That is why the message of this week is very important, and could lead to a big change in our attitude to God and our faith. Time spent reflecting on the passages from St Paul and Isaiah might help us to view things in a new and better way. Maybe our faith is a serious business, but it is also a happy, joyful one. As Isaiah says;

> *With joy you will draw water*
> *from the wells of salvation.*

And the promise he makes us is of a life filled with joy:

> *They will come to Zion shouting for joy,*
> *Everlasting joy on their faces;*
> *Joy and gladness will go with them*
> *And sorrow and lament will be ended.*

Hopefully, during these days, that note of joy will well up inside us and clear away the darkness.

8

PATIENT WAITING

Advent is a time of waiting. The dominant picture is of the child growing quietly and slowly in Mary's womb. In our part of the world Advent happens in winter, which is very appropriate. It happens at a time when the leaves have fallen from the trees, when the bare branches stand out starkly on the skyline, when the days are short, and the nights long, when the darkness has overpowered the day. But darkness is not always a negative image. At this time of the year the seed has returned to the earth, where it germinates slowly and silently, preparing itself for the bursting forth of Spring. It is resting and growing in the darkness. It contains within itself all the beauty of flowering and harvest. But it needs patient waiting. In the same way the child inside Mary is growing in the darkness, preparing himself for his bursting forth into light and life.

> *For as the earth makes fresh things grow,*
> *As a garden makes seeds spring up,*
> *So will the Lord God make both integrity and praise*
> *Spring up in the sight of the nations.*

It is hard for us to appreciate the beauty and wonder of all this, because we are living in an instant age – an age of instant food, instant communications. We have even tried to speed up nature. We pump our animals full of hormones so that they will grow more quickly.

We have hens living in twenty four-hour artificial light, so that they will lay twice as often as nature intended. We are using every method we can devise to manipulate and hasten the natural processes. But anyone who is familiar with the taste of a naturally produced egg, as against one that comes from forced feeding and laying, will know that there is a big price to be paid for all this impatience.

The really precious things in life refuse to be violated by speed. They have to take their natural course if they are to grow within us.

A loving relationship cannot be rushed. Some features come quickly, maybe even instantly; the excitement, the infatuation, possibly the sexual pleasure. But these early feelings, wonderful as they are, are not lasting. They have as yet no foundation. Real love grows slowly, through countless days of trying to understand, entering into the feelings of the other, reaching out from the depth of one's own self-centredness to focus on the other person, learning to place the needs of the other before one's own. This cannot happen quickly. It is slow, and often painful, learning. There are no short cuts. And that is why many relationships in the modern world do not last. People are not willing to wait. The Advent lesson of waiting is so important for the world.

In work we have been trained to look for instant success. So many of today's businesses are built on the notion of making quick profits. Young people are educated in the importance of being successful, in getting to the top. They learn to want it all now. But in life that does not usually happen. Work can be hard drudgery, the constant routine of repetitive events and tasks. For those who are looking for instant success, a sense of failure can set in quickly, and cripple their enthusiasm and their fragile feelings of self-worth. The Advent person, who knows how to be patient and to wait, can handle life better.

Even in our prayer life we can be infected by our need for instant answers. We want results, and we get impatient with God when nothing seems to be happening. But that is not God's way, as St Paul reminds us:

> With the Lord a day can mean a thousand years, and a thousand years is like a day…
> The Lord is being patient with us all, wanting nobody to be lost…

Suffering and sickness is the great school of patience, and it is a school that everyone will have to attend at some time in our lives. When that happens we lose control, things are taken out of our hands, and we must learn to let life take its course. Suffering is probably the biggest test that each one of us will have to endure. It can crush us, or it can make us great. It can be the time when we shrivel up in bitterness and despair, or when we grow into the fullness of our humanity. But we cannot grow without patient endurance. It is only very slowly that we begin to recognise the presence of God in our suffering. If we have come to know how to wait, to be patient, before the day of suffering comes, we will have a much greater chance of turning our time of suffering into the most beneficial time of our lives.

Joy, as we saw in the previous chapter, is a big theme of Advent: *I exult for joy in the Lord*

But it too cannot happen instantly. We may have great feeling of happiness, even of ecstasy. But real joy only comes through Advent waiting. Let us learn these days and weeks to open our hearts wide to joy, but to wait for its slow growth within us.

There is one other pitfall that can snare those who are waiting expectantly. The Jews were waiting for the coming of the Messiah, the Christ. They had been patient. They had waited for centuries, but had still kept their hope alive and vibrant. And now, as the Gospel tells us,

> A deep expectancy had grown up among them.

They sensed that the time was near.

But they made a dreadful mistake, one that we too can so easily make. Yes, they had expectations; they wanted a saviour. But they had made up their minds what type of saviour was needed. They wanted a political saviour to rescue them from the oppression of the Romans. And they wanted their saviour so badly that they did not recognise him when he came. This is a sobering, even a frightening, thought. These Jews were good people, deeply religious and prayerful. And yet they had fallen into the trap of wanting to control, wanting to have it their way. It is one of the greatest dangers of all. When we pray we know the answer we want. We have our lives all worked out, and we are sure of what is best. We get angry with God when he does not fall in with our plans. As a consequence, we so often fail to recognise the Saviour with us. He is working away in our lives, and we do not see him, because his plan is different to ours.

The attitude we must develop is one of openness to God, trying to learn his way.

> *Lord, make me know your ways.*
> *Lord, teach me your paths.*
> *Make me walk in your truth and teach me;*
> *For you are God, my saviour.*

We must come to trust him. As the prophet Jeremiah promises:

> *A ruler shall appear, one of themselves,*
> *A governor shall arise from their own number.*
> *I myself shall bring him near and so he shall approach me, says the Lord.*
> *So you shall be my people,*
> *And I will be your God.*

If we can learn these weeks the importance of patience, of waiting, then we will have learned one of the greatest lessons for life.

9

GOD GROWING IN US

From the moment Mary gave her word of approval to the angel an extraordinary thing began to happen in her. And yet it appeared so totally ordinary. A child was conceived, and began to develop. But this child was God. Mary, a young girl, began to give life to God. For the next nine months everything she did was contributing to the great project of bringing God into the world. It is an amazing thought, expressed beautifully in the writings of Caryll Houselander. Every meal she ate gave strength to God within her; every restful night restored the energy of the growing child; every breath she took brought the breath of life to God. God, the ultimate life-giver, was now dependent on the ordinary living of a young girl for his own life. For these nine months she folded in, cherishing the life within her, giving herself completely in order to bring him to life. She did it quietly, steadfastly, and with great patience.

In an equally extraordinary way, God grows in our lives too. It is not only in the lives of people who are particularly holy or good that God is at work, but in the lives of all of us, and of all people who are open to God in whatever way they perceive him. He is not a God who picks and chooses whom to love, but showers his gift of life and love on everyone who wishes to have it. And, just as happened with Mary during those nine months, he grows in us through the ordinary living of our lives. Again the image of the seed in winter is appropriate. It grows silently, most often in darkness, so that we cannot recognise what is happening. In the same way it is often only in retrospect that we can see the signs of his presence.

I am conscious of two things that are common in our lives, and that prove an obstacle to believing in the work of God, shaping us as the potter shapes the clay.

The first is our own sense of inadequacy, which leads us almost instinctively to believe that this could not be happening to us. 'I am not good enough, not holy enough, I don't pray properly'. But it wasn't because of the goodness of Mary that God worked such wonders for her. It was because the power of God came and rested on her. In the same way it is the power of God resting on us that brings him to life in us.

The second obstacle is our sense of guilt. Many of us are burdened with guilt. We feel bad and sinful, the sort of people that we think God would not want to be with. Because of the emphasis of the past this guilt can be most present with those who are struggling with any sort of sexual failure. To attempt to free ourselves from the crippling effects of these feelings we need to go back again to some of the wonderful passages we have been contemplating during the weeks of Advent:

> *Truly, God is my salvation,*
> *I trust, I shall not fear.*
> *For the Lord is my strength, my song,*
> *He became my saviour.*
> *With joy you will draw water*
> *From the wells of salvation.*

God has planned all of this for a definite purpose. Amazingly, he has put himself into a position where he needs us. He works through us. He needs our hands, so that he can heal. He needs our voice, so that he can speak words of comfort and support. He needs our feet so that he can go to the people and places that most cry out for him. He wants us to carry him in our hearts to places he cannot go without us, whether it is the factory, the school, visiting an old person, or whatever. He needs our love, so that he can love through us.

If God is alive in us, it doesn't matter whether we are contacting two people or two thousand, we are bringing his life. But we shouldn't be expecting to see miracles. Indeed it is better not to worry at all about the effect we have, about the results of our efforts or work. The values of God are different, and constantly challenge human values and standards. This is the wonderful message of Advent. Just as Christ came to life in the body of Mary, each one of us can also bring him to life in our lives. And bring him to life for others.

We need to trust that this is happening. And, like the natural cycle of growth in nature, we need to be patient and not rush his coming to life in us. Let it happen in his time.

How will people know that Christ is growing in us? Not by us appearing particularly holy or pious. The story of the visitation of Mary to Elizabeth gives a clue:

> Elizabeth gave a loud cry and said, 'Of all women you are the most blessed, and blessed is the fruit of your womb. Why should I be honoured with a visit from the mother of my Lord? For the moment your greeting reached my ears, the child in my womb leapt for joy'.

That is how it works. People will recognise the presence of God not by anything in us, but by an unfolding in themselves, a quickening of his life in their hearts. When God is at work the focus will not be on ourselves and our goodness. Rather it will be on the new life that comes from God, through us, to the other person. Christ is always present when people feel more alive; life generating life.

> I have come that you may have life; life in all its fullness.

10

TO SET US FREE

O key of David and sceptre of Israel, what you open no one else can close again; and what you close no one can open. O come to lead the captive from prison; free those who sit in darkness and in the shadow of death.

This notion of God as someone who frees us from captivity is important. There is a story in the Gospel of John that you are probably familiar with. It is the story of the raising of Lazarus from the dead. He was the brother of Martha and Mary, and a close friend of Jesus. He was in the tomb for four days before Jesus arrived. Still, the crowd gathered when they heard that the miracle worker had come. No doubt some were curious, wondering what he would do. Others were hopeful. They had never before seen anyone raised from the dead, but this man had mysterious powers. Maybe he even had power over death. When they went to the tomb, and Jesus asked that the stone covering the entrance be rolled away, the expectancy of the crowd must have been palpable. They all stood there in front of the open cave. It is likely that the body was visible inside, wrapped in the white shroud. The crowd must have been pressing around, anxious not to miss what would happen next. What Jesus did was wonderful in its simplicity. He called: 'Lazarus, come out!' The one who came to give life was standing face to face with death, and ordering it to free its captive. He was either possessed of powers never seen before, or else he was going to be shown up as a charlatan. This was a moment of truth. The story tells us that Lazarus responded to the summons and came out. Somewhere in the darkness he heard the call, and it stirred life in his deadness. Since his feet and hands were bound he certainly didn't walk out. He must have crawled, or rolled, out of that dark tomb, and presumably lay in a trussed up heap at Jesus' feet. The next words of Jesus are rich with meaning about his whole ministry and mission. He gestured towards Lazarus, and said to the people standing around: 'Unbind him, and let him go free'.

This notion of Jesus as someone who releases us from captivity, who has come to set us free is very prominent in the Advent readings. There are so many ways we can be held captive in this world. We can be captive to our past, carrying the hurts that have been done to us on our shoulders. There are people who never recover from feelings of inadequacy or failure that they learned early on in life. Maybe a teacher or a parent, or some other significant adult, told them that they were stupid, and they still believe it. Maybe they were abused, physically or sexually, as a child, and it has blighted their lives. They are full of resentment, and cannot forgive. Or maybe it is something they themselves have done, something about which they are full of shame and regret. The prisons, the tombs, the dark recesses that we can find ourselves locked into are many. But the one who is to come will set us free. He will call to us in exactly the same way that he called to Lazarus. He will call us to come out, to come out of the darkness into the light. This is the way Isaiah puts it:

O my people, do not be afraid. In that day the burden will depart from your shoulder and the yoke from your neck.

Or, in another place, he expresses it like this:

> *See, the King, the Lord of the earth is coming. He will take the burden of captivity from our shoulders.*

I have already referred to the sentence Jesus uses to express the same idea, but it is worth repeating again.

> *When that day comes, stand erect, hold your head high, because you liberation is at hand.*

When they cut the cloths that were binding Lazarus, he must have stood erect, delighting in his escape from the dark tomb, the captivity of death. There is a tendency to become a permanent victim in today's society. We often hear people say that because of something that was done to them their life was ruined, that they would never be happy again. 'My life was destroyed by that person,' they say. But the message of Advent is different. No matter what form of captivity we live under, we can be set free, free to live the fullness of life. God does not want anyone to live in captivity of any nature. The prophet Ezekiah puts it well:

> *I myself will pasture my sheep, I myself will show them where to rest. I shall look for the lost one, bring back the stray, bandage the wounded and make the weak strong.*
> *I will be a true shepherd to them.*

Sometimes in the Gospels, when Jesus met needy or sick people he asked them a question. He said: 'What do you want me to do for you?' It is a good question. We can learn to love our sickness, our hurt, our aggrieved feelings of victimhood. We can be so fragile, with so little sense of our own identity, that we actually need a grievance. The question from Jesus is simple and direct. Do we want to get well?

During these weeks of Advent, let us consciously let go of all forms of captivity, of slavery in all its manifestations. Let us hear his voice calling us to come out. Let us reach for the light, for a new and fuller existence. Let us stand erect as free people, holding our heads high. Our liberation is at hand.

Come, Lord Jesus; come and set us free.

11

THE MOUNTAIN
OF THE LORD

Carrantuohill is the highest mountain in Ireland. There are a number of different ways to climb it. On a showery, blustery day in the middle of a bad Irish summer I was climbing from Lough Acoose, a way that led over the peak of Caher mountain, and then along a narrow ridge to the final ascent to Carrantuohill. It had been a difficult climb, because the ground was wet and soft, and we were dragging our feet out of the bog. About three-quarters way up Caher we went into the cloud, so there was no view to lighten the drudgery of the climb. In the deepening mist we made our way along the ridge between the two peaks, walking carefully, and keeping our eyes focused on the next foothold. Then suddenly, and without warning, the mist cleared, and as if it was done purely for our benefit, we were presented with the most beautiful vista, a patchwork valley of sunshine and shadow laid out below us. We stopped, speechless and amazed. We had been up that mountain a number of times, but it had never appeared so beautiful to me as it did at that moment, emerging out of the mist. And then I knew, more deeply than ever before, the meaning of that passage from the prophet Isaiah:

> Come, let us go up to the mountain of the Lord,
> To the house of the God of Jacob;
> That he may teach us his ways and that we may walk in his paths.

There is something about being at the top of a mountain that gives a different perspective on life. The problems and difficulties are no longer so big, because you are viewing them from a distance. And the beauty and wonder of creation seem to diminish the often harsh reality of daily life.

Maybe you are not in the position to climb a high mountain. In our climate it would not be advisable to attempt it in the depths of winter. But it is possible to bring ourselves in spirit to 'the mountain of the Lord'. One of the features of life today is the prevalence of depression in all its different forms, and a dramatic increase in the incidence of suicide. That seems to imply that we are getting locked in to our problems, and that we haven't got the skills necessary to cope with life. Everything closes in around us, and we are swamped by it all. But if we can rise out of it, and climb that 'mountain of the Lord', he will give us a new perspective, a new way of looking at things. He will teach us his ways, and help us to walk in his paths.

He does not want us to be lost in depression or despair. On his mountain we will find Joy.

> *Go up on a high mountain, joyful messenger of Zion.*
> *Shout with a loud voice, joyful messenger of Jerusalem.*
> *Shout without fear; say to the towns of Judah,*
> *Here is your God.*

That is a wonderful image for our world; a person so full of joy that she wants to shout it out to the whole world.

Martin Luther King echoed this image, when he said: 'I've been to the mountain, and I've seen the Promised Land'.

And he was so full of joy at what he had seen that he wanted to tell the whole world. They put him to death, but that in no way inhibited his message, 'I have a dream ...'. He was inspired by the image of the Kingdom. If the wolf could lie down with the lamb, then surely coloured and white people could live in harmony. On the mountain he saw the vision of what could be, and he was fired by it.

The story of Advent is of a virgin giving birth to a child, and yet remaining a virgin. At the level of ordinary understanding this is nonsense. It just does not happen. In the human domain a woman cannot be a virgin and have a child. In this story we are confronted with the sheer unpredictability and strangeness of the actions of God. With God the impossible becomes possible, because he operates by different values. When people asked Jesus to heal them, he asked them to have faith. It is the same for us. If we have faith, anything is possible.

Let us go up to the mountain of the Lord, and begin to see things with the eyes of God. Then a new and beautiful vista will open up for us.

> On this mountain
> The Lord of hosts will prepare for all peoples
> A banquet of rich food, a banquet of fine wines,
> Of food rich and juicy, of fine strained wines.
> On this mountain he will remove
> The mourning veil covering all peoples,
> And the shroud enwrapping all nations,
> He will destroy death for ever.

The journey up the mountain of the Lord, which we are called to in Advent, is a journey well worth making.

12

O Rising Sun!

A loss of respect for the past is something of a characteristic of the age in which we live. Maybe it has to do with all the change we have experienced in our lifetime, but many people today tend to regard anything more than twenty-five years old as out of date. Some of the young generation look on older people as largely irrelevant. We live in a disposable age, when things are thrown out as soon as they give trouble. Those who can afford it change their car when it shows the first signs of wear and tear.

It would be a great pity if we began to treat all the culture, wisdom and knowledge that has come down to us through the generations in the same way. The French writer, Simone de Beauvoir, stated that a generation that turns its back on the wisdom of the past is making a big mistake. Despite our technological advances, human nature still remains essentially the same. We have the same weaknesses, and if we do not learn the lessons of the past we will inevitably repeat them. Any visit to, for instance, an art gallery or a library will quickly remind us of the wealth of artistic beauty which has been given to us by the generations that have gone before us.

Advent has been celebrated in the Church since the early days of Christianity. Around the seventh or eight centuries a series of seven antiphons were composed, expressing different themes of the season. They were very popular during the Middle Ages, but today are confined to the Prayer of the Church, as said mostly by priests and religious. The antiphons all have the same structure. Each one addresses God using a different title. Then they make a statement about him. And they end with a prayer, which begins with 'O come…'.

These O Antiphons, as they are called, are beautiful in themselves, and the thought that they have expressed the faith and longing of people for a thousand years or more gives us a sense of unity with our past.

Jesus as the wisdom of God is an image repeated many times in the Advent readings. The first antiphon picks up on that.

> O Wisdom, you come forth from the mouth of the Most High. You fill the universe and hold all things together in a strong yet gentle manner.
> O come to teach us the way of truth.

In the Old Testament story God appeared to Moses in a burning bush and spoke to him, asking him to lead his people out of slavery in Egypt to freedom in the Promised Land. This is an image of what is possible. Just as God sent a messenger to save the Israelites we now wait for the one who will save us.

> O Adonai and leader of Israel, you appeared to Moses in a burning bush and you gave him the law on Sinai. O come and save us with your mighty power.

Jesus came from a great kingly line. His ancestry can be traced back through King David to Jesse, his father. Because he came from a line of kings, kings are subservient to him. He is greater than them all.

> O stock of Jesse, you stand as a signal for the nations; kings fall silent before you whom the peoples acclaim. O come to deliver us, and do not delay.

The fourth antiphon takes up two of the great themes of Advent. Jesus is the one who leads us from captivity to freedom, from darkness to light.

> *O key of David, and sceptre of Israel, what you open no one else can close; what you close no one can open. O come to lead the captive from prison; free those who sit in darkness and in the shadow of death.*

The next one is probably the most beautiful of all, and speaks for itself. The coming of Jesus is like the sun rising in the east, dispelling the darkness of night. During these days immediately before Christmas we have the winter solstice. This is a celebration of the triumph of light over darkness. The sun rises on the shortest day, giving promise of the summer ahead. Jesus is our triumphant light.

> *O Rising Sun, you are the splendour of eternal light and the sun of justice. O come and enlighten those who sit in darkness and in the shadow of death.*

In the Gospel Jesus talked about how he was rejected, even by his own. But then he prophesied that the stone rejected by the builders would become the cornerstone, the key stone in the whole structure.

> *O King whom all the peoples desire, you are the cornerstone which makes all one. O come and save us whom you made from clay.*

The last of the antiphons, the one recited traditionally on Christmas Eve, uses the Bible name, Emmanuel, meaning God-with-us, for Jesus.

O Emmanuel, you are our king and judge, the One whom the peoples await and their Saviour. O come and save us, Lord our God.

You might not find these prayers very helpful at first. Maybe you are put off by the language or the images. But they are worth an effort. Any prayers that have lasted for so long, and that continue to be passed down through the generations, must speak to some deep areas of the human heart. Give them some time these weeks of Advent.

Come, Lord, and save us.

13

COME, MY LOVELY ONE

I hear my Beloved
See how he comes
Leaping on the mountains,
Bounding over the hills.
My beloved is like a gazelle,
Like a young stag.

This is an image and a language that the average Catholic is not
familiar with, at least not in a religious context. And yet it is from the
Bible, the Song of Songs. It is the reading for the Mass of 21
December. But, in order to protect people's sensibilities, there is an
alternative reading given for those who find this one too explicit.

The great painters of the Renaissance mostly used religious
themes in their paintings. But I am always struck by how sensuous is
their presentation of the bodies of the saints and Biblical figures.
People like St Jerome or Mary Magdalen are presented in all their
beauty and physicality. Clearly these artistic masters admired and
loved the human body, even in a deeply religious age. Obviously the
Catholic tradition of the recent past, which emphasised the
dichotomy between soul and body, and saw the body as the source of
sin and evil, was not always dominant in the Church. But it did shape
the attitudes of our generation towards sexuality, and all types of
physical expression. For many of us it was a struggle to accept our

physical selves, and to learn to be at home in our bodies. So, this passage from the Song of Songs, using the imagery of human love, even passion, to describe the one who is to come, might help free us from an excessive worry about our own bodily desires and passions.

> *My Beloved lifts up his voice,*
> *He says to me,*
> *'Come then, my love,*
> *my lovely one, come.'*

Imagine God speaking to us with that type of sensuous imagery, speaking to us with such affection and tenderness. God calling me 'my lovely one'! For most of us that is something we are not immediately at home with. He continues;

> *For see, winter is past,*
> *The rains are over and gone.*
> *The flowers appear on the earth.*
> *The season of glad songs has come,*
> *The cooing of the turtledove is heard in our land.*
> *The fig tree is forming its first figs*
> *And the blossoming vines give out their fragrance.*

This passage uses all the images that we have become familiar with from the writing of Isaiah. The Coming One, the One for whom we wait, will bring life, light, springtime and growth. It will be a time of joy and happiness. But this writer uses a very different type of language, and it may help to bring the message to life for us in a new way. The writer continues:

> *Come then, my love,*
> *My lovely one, come.*

My dove, hiding in the clefts of the rock,
In the coverts of the cliff,
Show me your face,
Let me hear your voice;
For your voice is sweet
And your face is beautiful.

For any one who has been in love, those lines will bring back memories. Maybe we have never been able to relate our experience of human love, and all the excitement that goes with it, to the love of God for us. What the writer of the Song of Songs is asking of us is precisely to make that connection. God is as passionate in his love for us as any human lover. He sees us as beautiful, he longs for our love, he desires and cries for our response. When we give our love to someone we put ourselves in a vulnerable position. The person we love may not respond, and we risk getting hurt. Amazingly, God does the same to us. As St John says in one of his letters:

It is not that we have loved God, but that he loved us…

And we know that his love will never fail. We may reject him, we may forget about him as we lose ourselves in the trivialities of life, but he will always be our passionate, loving God.

Maybe if you stay with these passages for a little while, and get some sense of the urgent, all-embracing love of God for you, you might gradually be able to address the same sentiments to him in return. You might be able to say to God:

Come then, my love,
My lovely one, come.

14

Characters in the Christmas Story

The Christmas story has caught the imagination of people, young and old, for two thousand years. Whither we understand it to be myth, or literal truth, or a combination of both – which is the most likely – it still has the power to lead us out of ourselves, and our material world, into a world of wonder and mystery. I think the core of the story is summed up in the words of the angel to the shepherds on that night:

> *I bring you tidings of great joy, a joy to be shared by all the people.*

The story of Christmas is first and foremost a story of joy for the whole of humanity. A new life, a life that is available to everyone, has come into the world.

It might help to add freshness to the story if we can use our imagination to flesh out some of the characters of that night. What might they have been thinking to themselves as the events unfolded? Let's give them a voice, a chance to explain themselves.

The innkeeper was one of the characters who come badly out of the story as it has been passed down to us. He turned away the Holy Family. The fact that there was no way he could have known who was at his door tends to be overlooked. Maybe the bad press we have given him is not totally fair. Let's hear what he has to say.

The Innkeeper:

I'm fed up of all this! Two thousand years of bad-mouthing, slandering my good name! And smug people sitting in church pews thinking how awful I was to turn away the Saviour, and how they would have behaved so differently if they had been in my situation. Yes, I suppose they would have put out the red carpet, and given him the best room in the house! But, would they?

How was I supposed to know who was at my door? This was the biggest night of the year for me. Because of the census, people were flocking in from all sides, everyone looking for a room. There just weren't enough beds in the town for all the visitors. I could charge whatever I liked. It was my chance to make a bit of money, to make up for all the quiet nights when my hotel was almost empty.

And this couple was obviously poor. They couldn't pay the sort of money others were throwing at me. And she about to give birth. I had no way of knowing who the child was to be. I didn't want that sort of bother on this of all nights.

I didn't close the door on them. I told them where they could find a stable. It seemed to me that was where they belonged, not in my good hotel with well-off people clamouring to get in.

I would have thought that people in the twenty-first century would understand my actions. After all, you have become fairly skilled at making money yourselves, haven't you?

Mary was the one who knew more than anyone what was the significance of that night. She had experienced the visit from the angel. What must that night have been like for her? Maybe it was something like this.

Mary:

That was an anxious time for me. I was young, and while I still remembered clearly the visit of the angel to ask me to do God a favour, sometimes I wondered if it had all been a dream.

But mostly I wondered what this child would be like. I had been told he would be special, that he had a great destiny ahead of him, that he would achieve great things. Would I be able to measure up to the task? Giving birth was one thing; rearing him would be a much more difficult task entirely.

So, I was full of anxiety.

But when the child came, and when I held him in my arms, hugged him close to me, I knew it would be all right, that everything would be OK I just felt surrounded by love. As I was holding the child it seemed as if God was holding me. All my fears and anxieties left me, and I was at peace.

It must have been a troubled night for Joseph also. We don't know much about his life, or the type of man he was. The Gospels tell us so little. Some scholars today speculate about him. Because of the references in the Gospels to the brothers and sisters of Jesus, they wonder if Joseph might not have been married before, and been left a widower with young children. Maybe he married Mary in order to have a mother for his children, so that the one's referred to, including the apostles James and John, could have been Jesus' half brothers. We have no way of knowing for certain. But let us assume, just for the moment, that this is correct, and try to enter into his mind on the night.

Joseph:
I was certainly troubled that night. It was the night that really tested my faith. Some of my friends had warned me that I was making a big mistake in marrying this young girl, that there was too big a gap in our ages. But I needed someone to look after my kids when my first wife died. And Mary seemed such a nice girl. That was until she came and told me that she was pregnant. I couldn't believe she would do something like that. And the

fantastic story she told me about a visit from an angel, and God being the father. Would you have believed that story? I can tell you, I found it hard to swallow.

But that night, after she gave birth, I no longer had any doubts. I can't explain it. I just knew the child was special, destined to be great, and that her story was true. To see the way she welcomed him, held him, looked at him; it was like nothing I had ever seen before. I was both happy and frightened. How would I cope with all this? What was ahead of me?

From that moment on my life was different.

There was a lot about that night that was peculiar and unpredictable. God's ways were certainly strange. But one of the most extraordinary aspects of the story was the people to whom he chose to announce the coming of the Saviour. As the Gospel puts it, 'some shepherds out minding their sheep'. Not exactly the important people of the time. What might those shepherds have thought when the message came to them in such a spectacular fashion?

Shepherd:
That was an extraordinary night. I will never forget it. I was a shepherd, a simple man living with my sheep. I was of no importance, had no education, no influence, not even many friends except the sheep. I didn't expect anyone to announce anything to me, especially something as important as the coming of a Saviour. If I were God I'd have gone to the Emperor in Rome with my news.

But I can still sometimes hear the singing of the angels; it was like nothing I had ever heard before. 'Tidings of great joy for all peoples,' they said to me.

When I got to the stable all I saw was a poor couple with a new-born baby. How could this little child save anyone? But there was something mysterious about the place. I just stood there inside the door. Seeing the animals made me feel more at home. I gradually began to sense that the scene before me was important, that someone had come into the world, and nothing would ever be the same again.

I went back to the hills with my sheep, and I was never the same again either. I couldn't forget the sound of the singing ...

Herod, the King of Judea, was another person for whom that night had considerable significance. We know that his response to the night was to do a terrible thing, to slaughter innocent babies. Could we get into his mind, and find out why he might have responded the way he did?

Herod:
I was in a very difficult position. I was the king of Judea, but I didn't have the sort of power that my ancestors had. Not since the Romans had taken over. Now I was always looking over my shoulder, not wanting to draw unwelcome attention to myself. Anything that might have smacked of rebellion would have been big trouble for me.

I was a Jew myself, and I knew all about the Messiah that was supposed to be coming. I didn't really believe in any of it, of course, but it worried me all the same. You see, in the past it had been a harmless dream indulged in by the more pious people – it actually helped to keep them quiet – but in recent years it had hardened into a belief that a political leader would come and drive out the Romans. That was the last thing I wanted. If a rebellion started, both sides would turn on me.

So, when I heard all this talk about a child having been born – the promised Saviour – I was terrified. I had to act before things got out of hand. And if that meant killing a few innocent kids, so what. People are expendable; sometimes you have to take drastic action for the common good. Hard luck on the kids! But that's life! Would anybody else have done differently in my situation? I don't think so.

Clearly the different characters of the Christmas story were all human, some of them weak and fragile, others selfish. Probably a lot like the rest of us. And yet God used them to bring about the 'message of great joy for all peoples'. What messages of great joy has he planned for us to bring into the world?

15

THE LIGHT HAS COME

While they were there the time came for her to have her child, and she gave birth to a son, her first-born. She wrapped him in swaddling clothes, and laid him in a manger because there was no room for them at the inn.

The readings for the Masses on Christmas Day are full of confirmation that what we have hoped for has come, and that all our expectations are going to be fulfilled. If you have given some time during the weeks of Advent to waiting patiently, and reflecting on the meaning of his coming, then this day is bound to mean more to you. It is a day to celebrate. But not just in the sense that we normally associate Christmas celebration. This is celebration at a much deeper level entirely.

> *The people that walked in darkness*
> *Has seen a great light;*
> *On those who live in a land of deep shadow*
> *A light has shone.*
> *You have made their gladness greater,*
> *You have made their joy increase.*

No longer will we live in darkness; no longer will we inhabit the land of deep shadow. The light has come, and it can never be put out. In the best possible sense, nothing will ever be the same again. Now that we have glimpsed the light, we cannot return to the darkness. We must learn to live by the light. This involves change, change of outlook and lifestyle. And that can be painful. But, having seen the light, we are drawn to the wonder of it. T.S. Eliot expresses how the Magi, the three wise kings who came to visit the infant, felt in 'The Journey of the Magi'. The new way of looking at things shown up by the light involved letting go of so much of their past that they wondered whither it was birth or death they had witnessed.

> *All this was a long time ago, I remember,*
> *And I would do it again, but set down*
> *This set down*
> *This: were we led all that way for*
> *Birth or Death? There was a Birth, certainly,*
> *We had evidence and no doubt. I had seen birth and death,*
> *But had thought they were different; this Birth was*
> *Hard and bitter agony for us, like Death, our death.*
> *We returned to our places, these Kingdoms,*
> *But no longer at ease here, in the old dispensation,*
> *With an alien people clutching their gods.*
> *I should be glad of another death.*

For us too there is both birth and death. Living a new life, seeing things in a new way, involves giving up many of our old ways. This is not easy. But, like the Magi in the poem, there is no going back. Not only have we seen the light; we have also gone to the mountain, the mountain of the Lord, and from that perspective we have learned that the new life is the only one worth living. From our eyrie on the mountain, with the sharp vision of the golden eagle, we have seen the messenger coming.

> *How beautiful on the mountains*
> *Are the feet of one who brings good news,*
> *Who heralds peace, brings happiness,*
> *Proclaims salvation,*
> *And tells Zion,*
> *'Your God is king'.*

A new age has dawned, an age in which peace, happiness and salvation are now more possible than ever before.

> *God's grace has been revealed, and it has made salvation possible for the whole human race.*

Or Isaiah:

> *The Lord bares his holy arm*
> *In the sight of all the nations*
> *And all the ends of the earth shall see*
> *The salvation of our God.*

This is wonderful news, and Isaiah suggests to us how we might respond;

> *Break into shouts of joy together,*
> *You ruins of Jerusalem;*
> *For the Lord is consoling his people,*
> *Redeeming Jerusalem.*

And maybe one last expression of the same sentiments, this time from the beginning of St John's Gospel. He is writing about the Messiah, Jesus, whom he calls the Word of God.

All that came to be had life in him
And that life was the light of all peoples,
A light that shines in the dark,
A light that darkness could not overpower.

Jesus is the Life-giver, he is the Light of the world, he is the one who has come to set us free.